in
the
news™

DOPING

ATHLETES
AND DRUGS

Jason Porterfield

ROSEN
PUBLISHING®
New York

Published in 2008 by The Rosen Publishing Group, Inc.
29 East 21st Street, New York, NY 10010

Library of Congress Cataloging-in-Publication Data

Porterfield, Jason.
Doping: athletes and drugs / Jason Porterfield.—1st ed.
   p. cm.—(In the news)
ISBN-13: 978-1-4042-1917-5 (hardcover)
ISBN-10: 1-4042-1917-X (hardcover)
1. Doping in sports. 2. Athletes—Drug use. I. Title.
RC1230.P68 2008
362.29
                        2007015919

Manufactured in the United States of America

On the cover: *(Clockwise from top right)* An employee working in the Olympics Doping Center laboratory during the 2004 games in Athens, Greece; fans express their thoughts on the state of professional baseball during the 2002 All-Star Game at Miller Park in Milwaukee, Wisconsin; on March 17, 2005, Mark McGwire *(left)* and Rafael Palmeiro listen as Curt Schilling is sworn in on Capitol Hill, Washington, D.C., during the House Committee hearings investigating Major League Baseball.

contents

Recent Doping Scandals

I n many sports, physical traits such as power, speed, and endurance are highly prized. Today's athletes follow strength, conditioning, and nutrition programs to help them stay in shape through long sports seasons. These regimens may be designed to help them maintain their edge. Some athletes might work around old injuries or try to improve skills that have declined. Other athletes will try to make themselves stronger, faster, and more agile.

However, some of them get impatient with training sessions or aren't satisfied with the results. They may look for other ways to take their abilities to a higher level. These athletes may turn to doping, or using drugs designed to enhance their performance. Doping can occur in many forms, from using steroids or human growth hormone (HGH) to build muscle mass, to taking amphetamines to maintain stamina in endurance sports. To most fans and "clean" athletes, doping is cheating.

Doping occurs in countless sports at both the professional and amateur levels. Many Olympic sports like skiing, wrestling, and weight lifting are monitored closely for doping. Some sports, such as track and field and professional cycling, have long had rigorous testing systems. Professional football and hockey have required player testing for years. Major League Baseball, however, failed to respond quickly or efficiently to doping allegations.

Major League Baseball and Doping

Perhaps the highest-profile doping cases have been occurring in Major League Baseball. The use of performance-enhancing drugs by baseball players has been an issue in the major leagues for decades. Players allegedly began using amphetamines during the 1960s to stay alert during games. Throughout the late 1970s and early 1980s, players' use of cocaine during games was widespread. A grand jury investigation regarding evidence of cocaine use by members of the 1985 Pittsburgh Pirates team and other major leaguers led to a number of suspensions during the 1986 baseball season. In 1991, Major League Baseball finally instituted a ban on controlled substances (drugs, many of which were illegal, that could affect player performance on the field), including steroids. However, the organization did not implement any system for testing players.

McGwire, Sosa, and Bonds: Breaking Baseball Records

Through the record-breaking offensive seasons spanning the 1990s, suspicions began to surface that players might be using steroids to artificially inflate their home-run totals. The 1998 home-run race between Mark McGwire of the St. Louis Cardinals and Sammy Sosa of the Chicago Cubs made history. Both sluggers broke Roger Maris's 1961 single-season record of sixty-one home runs. McGwire established the new record with seventy homers, while Sosa hit sixty-six. After Maris and Babe Ruth, they became just the third and fourth players in major league history to hit more than sixty home runs in a season. The two were hailed as heroes and credited with reawakening the public's interest in baseball. During the 1999 season, McGwire and Sosa hit sixty-five and sixty-three home runs, respectively. In 2001, Sosa hit sixty-four home runs, becoming the first major league player to hit more than sixty homers in three seasons.

Both Sosa and McGwire were muscular and attributed their bulk to exercise. Though McGwire had always been big, Sosa was once a slender, speedy outfielder. During the 1998 season, McGwire admitted to using a performance-enhancing prohormone, androstenedione, which was not banned at the time.

In 2001, San Francisco Giants outfielder Barry Bonds finished the season with seventy-three homers, shattering

Mark McGwire, above, watches the ball after he hit his seventieth home run in September 1998. Although he became a hero to many fans during his record-setting season, rumors that he may have used steroids during his playing career have since tarnished his legacy.

McGwire's mark. Bonds had long been considered one of the best players in baseball, with a rare combination of speed and power. By 2001, he had developed a much larger, more muscular physique, which he attributed to hours spent training in the gym.

Unlike McGwire and Sosa, however, Bonds had a reputation as a moody player who often clashed with the media. The public became skeptical of Bonds's record. Maris's record had stood for thirty-seven years before McGwire broke it, whereas McGwire's own record lasted only three seasons. Despite allegations, Bonds denied that he used performance-enhancing drugs.

Though no seventy-home-run seasons have thus far followed Bonds's record-setting year, home run totals have remained high. Before 1990, only fourteen players had *ever* hit more than fifty home runs in a season. Since 1990, eighteen players have accomplished the feat. Smaller ballparks, a decline in pitching talent, and the exercise regimens of modern players all have been cited as possible factors in the offensive explosion. After all, early sluggers like Babe Ruth didn't lift weights or pay attention to what they ate. It even has been suggested that changes in the way manufacturers make baseballs are responsible for players hitting so many home runs.

Admissions of Steroid Use and the BALCO Case

In 2002, just a year after Bonds's record-setting season, former major league player Ken Caminiti revealed to *Sports Illustrated* magazine that he had used steroids during his career. (Caminiti, ravaged by years of substance abuse, died of a suspected overdose in 2004.) The span of his steroid use included 1996, the year he was named the National League's Most Valuable Player (MVP). Though some players had been suspected of using steroids, this was the first time one ever admitted to it.

In 2003, Bonds's trainer, Greg Anderson of the Bay Area Laboratory Co-operative (BALCO), was indicted by a federal grand jury on charges that his company provided steroids to athletes. Though the court agreed to conceal the names of the athletes—including major league players Barry Bonds and Jason Giambi—from the press, their testimony was leaked. Bonds denied that he knowingly used steroids. Giambi, a first baseman for the New York Yankees and a former MVP for the Oakland Athletics, admitted to steroid use in his testimony. The information was reported in the *San Francisco Chronicle* by Mark Fainaru-Wada and Lance Williams, who later expanded their coverage into the book *Game of Shadows: Barry Bonds, BALCO, and the Steroid Scandal That Rocked Professional Sports*. Players themselves fueled the steroid discussion by making allegations in their own books and statements to the media. In his 2005 autobiography, *Juiced: Wild Times, Rampant 'Roids, Smash Hits, and How Baseball Got Big*, former baseball player and MVP-award-winner José Canseco admitted to steroid use. He also singled out other celebrated players as users, including McGwire, Giambi, Bonds, and Baltimore Orioles slugger Rafael Palmeiro. The book spurred the U.S. government to hold hearings investigating steroid abuse in baseball.

Seven prominent former and current baseball players—Giambi, Sosa, Palmeiro, Canseco, McGwire, two-time MVP Frank Thomas, and All-Star pitcher Curt

(From left to right) José Canseco, Sammy Sosa, Mark McGwire, Rafael Palmeiro, and Curt Schilling, some with their lawyers, sit before a congressional committee on March 17, 2005. Their testimony about steroids was part of an extensive federal investigation into drug use in sports.

Schilling—were subpoenaed to appear before Congress. Baseball commissioner Bud Selig and Donald Fehr of the Major League Baseball Players Association (MLBPA) also appeared. As a result of the hearings, Congress appointed former senator George Mitchell to serve as a special investigator into allegations of steroid use in baseball.

Drug Testing in Major League Baseball

Major League Baseball had begun random drug testing in 2003, but the results were kept confidential and there were no penalties. More than 5 percent of test samples taken that season came back positive, so anonymous tests were also performed in 2004. After the congressional hearings, however, penalties were put into place. Beginning in 2005, a positive test resulted in a ten-game suspension. A player would be suspended thirty games for a second offense, and sixty for a third. If he tested positive a fourth time, he would be suspended for one year. All suspensions were without pay.

Twelve major league players tested positive for steroids and received suspensions during the 2005 season. Perhaps the most widely publicized among them was Baltimore Oriole Rafael Palmeiro, who had vehemently denied using steroids when he testified before Congress. Palmeiro's positive test, for the anabolic steroid stanozolol, was announced August 1, 2005. Shortly after returning from his ten-game suspension, his team benched him. Palmeiro, who had collected more than 3,000 hits and 500 home runs throughout a twenty-year career and was considered a possible Hall of Famer, hasn't played since.

Before the 2006 season began, Major League Baseball and the MLBPA bowed to pressure from Congress, agreeing to test for steroid use throughout the season and implement tougher penalties. Players testing positive would be suspended for 50 games for a first offense and 100 games for a second. They would be banned from baseball for life after a third positive test.

In addition, 2006 was the first year that Major League Baseball tested for amphetamines. If a player tests positive, more testing and treatment serve as penalties. As with the earlier steroid tests, results were supposed to remain confidential. However, news that Barry Bonds had tested positive for amphetamines leaked to the press. Though Bonds tested positive only once and wasn't punished, the incident further damaged a reputation already marred by allegations of steroid use.

The Jason Grimsley Raid

During the 2006 season, federal agents raided the home of Arizona Diamondbacks pitcher Jason Grimsley after he received a shipment of HGH through the mail. Grimsley was suspended for fifty games but was released from the team before completing his suspension.

In Grimsley's home, investigators found information on a widespread network of people selling performance-enhancing drugs, mostly steroids and HGH. Grimsley agreed to cooperate with the investigation. The media has speculated that names of other athletes who have purchased performance-enhancing drugs from the same network could become public.

Federal investigators also took data from Major League Baseball's confidential steroids tests from 2003. The scientific capability exists to match players with the samples. Though judges have ruled that this information cannot be released to the public, players worry that the information could be leaked.

To date, only two Major League Baseball players have been officially banned from baseball for life due to drug use. Starting pitcher Ferguson Jenkins was banned in 1980, and relief pitcher Steve Howe was banned in 1992, both for using cocaine. They eventually were reinstated, however, allowing Jenkins to be elected to the Hall of Fame in 1991 and Howe to continue his once-promising career. Howe retired in 1996. Sadly, he was killed in a traffic accident in 2006. The drug methamphetamine was found in his system.

Doping and the Tour de France

Doping in cycling has been a frequent news topic in recent times. The grueling Tour de France, which began in 1903, is the premier international cycling event. The race lasts for twenty-three days and covers between 1,800 and 2,400 miles (2,897 to 3,862 kilometers) through the French Alps and countryside. In order to excel in the race, cyclists require superhuman strength, speed, and stamina. Cyclists compete in teams of nine and must be in peak physical shape to be selected by a team.

Unlike baseball, professional cycling has long had rigorous testing procedures and regulations to guard against doping. Early in the tour's history, riders would

Tommy Simpson was Great Britain's first world cycling champion. Above, he cycles in a Milan race, seven years before his death at the Tour de France.

drink alcohol or use ether gas to dull their aches and pains. Instead of deadening their senses, later riders started using drugs, such as amphetamines, that elevated their performances. In 1967, British cyclist Tommy Simpson died from taking amphetamines while competing in the tour. Despite his death, and the fact that the UCI (Union Cycliste Internationale, or International Cyclist's Union) started testing for performance-enhancing drugs in 1966 and began applying penalties in 1967, drug use continued.

"Tour of Shame" and Tougher Testing Measures

During the 1998 Tour de France, a stash of illegal drugs and equipment was discovered in the possession of managers and health officials for the Festina and TVM teams. Willy Voet, a trainer for the Festina team, was arrested for possession of testosterone, HGH, and amphetamines. In response, riders staged a strike during the tour's seventeenth stage and many teams quit the race. In the end, only 96 of the 189 riders completed the 1998 "Tour of Shame."

The Festina scandal led to tougher testing measures and the creation of the World Anti-Doping Agency (WADA) in 1999. Still, doping persisted. In 2004, cyclists Phillipe Gaumont and David Millar of the Confidis team admitted that doping was widespread on their team. Millar confessed to using erythropoietin (EPO), an illegal means of increasing endurance. The same year, rider Jesus Manzano of the Kelme team revealed that his team had forced him to take performance-enhancing drugs.

In August 2005, the French sports paper *L'Equipe* charged Lance Armstrong with doping to win his first Tour de France. The front-page article headline reads "The Armstrong Lie."

Doping allegations were brought against American cyclist Lance Armstrong by the French sports newspaper *L'Équipe* in 2005, soon after Armstrong's record seventh consecutive tour win. The paper claimed that Armstrong used EPO during his first tour victory in 1999, a charge that Armstrong has denied. In response, the UCI launched an investigation that found that the WADA had been inconsistent in following anti-doping rules.

Doping Charges Continue to Haunt the Tour

In 2006, doping charges plagued the tour even before it began. Seventeen riders were implicated in Spain's Operación Puerto investigation. All seventeen were barred from competition, including top cyclists Ivan Basso and Jan Ullrich, who had won the tour in 1997.

American Floyd Landis, the winner of the 2006 tour, had not been favored to win. Four days after the finish of the race, the UCI revealed that Landis had tested positive for a testosterone imbalance after winning the seventeenth stage. Far back in the pack, he had made a stunning comeback during the stage, winning it easily. As of this writing, the UCI has not stripped him of the victory, and Landis has said that he will fight to clear his name.

Doping and the Olympics

Doping allegations have surrounded the Olympic Games since their modern inception in 1896. British marathoner Thomas J. Hicks won a gold medal in 1904 after his coach dosed him with alcohol and a poisonous chemical called strychnine. In 1952, the Soviet weight-lifting team was suspected of doping. So was Soviet runner Vladimir Kuts, the winner of the gold medal in the 5,000 and 10,000 meter races at the 1956 Olympics. Amphetamine use contributed to the death of Danish cyclist Knud Enemark Jensen during the 1960 Olympics in Rome.

The Olympics' Doping Ban

The International Olympic Committee (IOC) banned doping in 1967, following cyclist Tommy Simpson's death in the Tour de France. During the 1968 games, Swedish pentathlete Hans-Gunnar Liljenwall was the first Olympic athlete to test positive for drug use. He was stripped of his bronze medal for using alcohol, a substance banned by the IOC for its pain-numbing properties. Since then, seventy-three athletes have been disqualified from the games after testing positive. One of these athletes was Canadian sprinter Ben Johnson. Johnson won the gold medal in the 100-meter sprint at the 1988 Olympics, setting a new world record. His medal and record were stripped from him, however, after he tested positive for the steroid stanozolol. German freestyle wrestler Alexander Leipold also was stripped of his gold medal during the 2000 Summer Games. In the 2002 Winter Olympics, medals were stripped from several athletes, including Russian cross-country skiers Olga Danilova and Larissa Lazutina.

At the 2006 Winter Games, officials raided the rooms of the Austrian cross-country ski team after learning that biathalon coach Walter Mayer was present. Mayer had been banned from participating in all Olympic Games through 2010 because of an earlier doping charge. Mayer fled the premises with two of the skiers, Wolfgang Rottmann and Wolfgang Perner. Rottmann and Perner later told officials that they may have used banned substances.

Doping and American Track and Field

American runners Marion Jones, Tim Montgomery, and Justin Gatlin have all been accused of using performance-enhancing drugs. Jones had won five medals at the 2000 Olympics, but in 2005 she became caught up in the same BALCO scandal

Ben Johnson celebrates after winning the gold medal and setting a world record in the 100-meter sprint at the 1988 Summer Olympics. He later tested positive for steroids.

as Barry Bonds. In addition, her ex-husband, Olympic shot-putter and admitted steroid user C. J. Hunter, alleged that Jones injected steroids before and during the Olympics. Jones has denied the charges. Since she never tested positive for the drugs, she has kept her medals.

Tim Montgomery won a gold medal in the 2000 Olympics as a member of the 400-meter relay team. In 2002, he went on to set a world record for the 100-meter sprint. Shortly before the qualifying races for the 2004 Summer Olympics, the U.S. Anti-Doping Agency charged Montgomery with using performance-enhancing drugs. He performed poorly in the qualifiers, failing to make the Olympic team. Montgomery didn't test positive but allegedly had received steroids and HGH from BALCO. In 2005, he was banned from track competitions for two years and stripped of all of his results, awards, records (including his world record), and winnings dating from March 31, 2001, to November 30, 2003.

Justin Gatlin was also an Olympic gold medalist, winning the 100-meter sprint at the 2004 Summer Games. Like Montgomery, Gatlin followed up his success at the Olympics with the setting of a world record. In May 2006, he tied Jamaican sprinter Asafa Powell's record in the 100-meter sprint. Two months later, however, Gatlin was informed that he tested positive for a performance-enhancing drug, believed to be testosterone. A second test confirmed the result. Technically, this was Gatlin's second positive test. He had tested positive for amphetamines in 2001 and was banned from competition for two years. However, the disciplinary committee lifted that ban early after Gatlin argued that the positive test came about because of medication he had taken for years. He could have been banned for life after his second positive test. Ultimately, Gatlin agreed to an eight-year ban from track and field.

Doping: Looking for an Edge

A thletes constantly are looking for ways to improve. They may switch to a different exercise regimen or spend time focusing on an aspect of their performance that gives them trouble. They may try a different diet if they feel it gives them more energy. They also might begin a regimen of sports supplements, which are legal and permitted in many sports. In a worst-case scenario, an athlete who becomes impatient with exercise and practice may start experimenting with performance-enhancing drugs, ignoring the dangers in favor of what he or she sees as a quick and easy way to success.

A Brief History of Doping

It is likely that as long as human beings have engaged in athletic competition, athletes have sought shortcuts to peak performance. The very word "dope" is probably derived from the Dutch "dop," an alcoholic beverage that traditional Zulu warriors of South Africa would drink before competitions. Historical records reveal that thousands of years ago, fighters and athletes took substances believed to enhance performance. In ancient Greece, where a victory in the Olympics led to fame and wealth, athletes restricted their diets and drank preparations of mushrooms and herbs to give themselves an advantage in competition. Roman gladiators sometimes ingested wine infused with medicinal plants. South American natives have long chewed the leaves of the coca plant, from which cocaine is derived, for its stimulant properties.

In the nineteenth century, cycling races became immensely popular in Europe. Cyclists dosed themselves with a range of dangerous substances such as strychnine, cocaine, nitroglycerine, digitalis, and heroin in order to enhance their performance. The first death attributed to doping occurred in 1896, when a Welsh cyclist, Andrew Linton, overdosed on trimethyl. Use of performance-enhancing substances spread to other sports, including swimming, ice skating, and boxing. During the 1904 Olympics, American runner Thomas Hicks won the marathon but collapsed after crossing the finish line. During the course of the race, his trainers had twice dosed him with mixtures of strychnine and brandy, which acted as a stimulant. One more dose would likely have proven fatal.

Assistants cool runner Thomas Hicks with damp sponges at the twenty-third mile of the 1904 Olympic marathon. He won the race but nearly died from the mixture of alcohol and strychnine that he used.

Doping in the Twentieth Century

New scientific discoveries in the twentieth century led to great advances in medicine. This progress, however, also made possible a new era of doping. Scientists isolated the animal form of the male sex hormone testosterone in 1921, and the human form in 1931. In 1935, a chemist succeeded in producing a synthetic form. German athletes participating in the 1936 Olympics took testosterone to boost their performance. Throughout World War II

(1939–1945), both American and German soldiers used the stimulant amphetamine, which was first marketed in 1932. During the 1940s and 1950s, the first anabolic steroids were developed.

During the Cold War, competition in sports events was particularly fierce between the United States and the Soviet Union. Throughout the 1950s, due to drugs such as testosterone, Soviet weight lifters dramatically improved their performance. Some Americans came to believe that unless U.S. athletes began regimens of performance-enhancing drugs, they would be unable to compete successfully with the Soviets. Therefore, the sports physician John Ziegler collaborated with a pharmaceutical company to develop an even more effective drug. The anabolic steroid that resulted from their work—marketed as Dianabol—quickly became popular with athletes. Serious physical and psychological side effects soon became evident, however, including high blood pressure, liver damage, and dramatic mood swings. As a result, Ziegler came to regret participating in the project.

Steroid use continued to spread to a variety of other sports during this time. Due to the danger and questionable ethics of performance-enhancing drugs, the International Olympic Committee (IOC) released a list of prohibited substances in 1967. Reliable drug tests, however, were not available until the 1976 Olympics.

East German swimmer Kornelia Ender won four gold and two silver medals at the 1976 Olympics. Her trainers allegedly gave her steroids without her knowledge.

The new rules and testing procedures did not put an end to the popularity of performance-enhancing drugs. In the 1976 Olympics, members of the East German women's swim team won eleven out of thirteen possible gold medals. Years later, archived records revealed that scientists had devised a means for them to cheat the drug test. These East German women had been part of a vast government-supported doping program. Promising athletes were singled out at a young age and administered drugs, sometimes without their knowledge. Doctors would claim that they were just vitamins or nutritional supplements. The young female swimmers began exhibiting severe side effects, such as deep voices and excess body hair. For some, the long-term physical and psychological conse-quences of the drug regimen devastated their lives.

Today, performance-enhancing drugs continue to be an issue of grave concern within the sports world.

Every year, world-class athletes are disqualified from their sports for doping, often amid scandal.

Why Do They Cheat?

Most athletes know about the negative consequences of using performance-enhancing drugs. The health risks of steroids and other doping agents have been well publicized. A positive drug test can destroy an athlete's career and tarnish his or her legacy. Ben Johnson, for example, is remembered most not for his athletic accomplishments but for the stunning revelation of his steroid use.

On top of the immediate consequences, athletes face the ethical considerations of doping. To millions of fans, professional athletes serve as role models. They also provide fans with a feeling that they are personally connected to the sport. When these larger-than-life figures are exposed as drug users, it often causes controversy and elicits a variety of reactions. Some fans feel so betrayed that the entire sport is diminished in their eyes. On the other hand, for some aspiring athletes, frequent and widespread drug use among professionals sends the message that it is acceptable behavior.

What makes professional athletes decide that the advantages of performance-enhancing drugs outweigh the risks? Part of the incentive is the money and prestige available to world-class athletes. The best athletes are paid astronomical salaries. They make even more money from lucrative endorsement deals for everything from sports gear to cereal. A veteran athlete may see steroids and other drugs as a way to extend a successful career. An ambitious younger athlete may view them as a way to break into the major leagues. For some sports, such as many track and field events, just a fraction of a second can separate the winner from the runner-up. At the highest levels, this split-second advantage may lead the gold medalist to endorsement deals worth millions of dollars, as well as international recognition. With such mind-boggling rewards for winning, the temptation to cheat is high.

Athletes Feel the Pressure

It is easy to condemn individual athletes for their actions when it comes to doping, but there is considerable pressure in the sports world to excel at any cost. Fans are eager to see athletes set records and compete in high-suspense games. In an age where physical enhancements such as cosmetic surgery and Botox are becoming mainstream, athletes often feel that they must take any steps possible to eliminate physical limitations or keep up with younger, stronger players. When use of steroids and other performance-enhancing drugs is widespread in a sport, an athlete may feel that he or she has no

American track and field coach Trevor Graham was deeply involved with BALCO. Many of his athletes, such as Marion Jones, won Olympic medals only to be implicated in drug scandals.

choice but to turn to drugs in order to be able to compete with the drug-enhanced athletes.

Coaches and managers add to the pressure to perform. It is a coach's job to demand the best from his or her athletes. In some circumstances, a desperate athlete may resort to doping in order to fulfill these expectations. In a few cases, coaches have been directly implicated in their athletes' drug use. Trevor Graham coached a number of track and field champions, including Olympic medalists Marion Jones, Antonio Pettigrew, Jerome Young, and twin brothers Calvin and Alvin Harrison. He has become the center of controversy, though, as eight of his athletes

Don Hooton *(above)* became an activist for steroid testing after his seventeen-year-old son committed suicide. Many former steroid users become severely depressed after they stop doping.

have tested positive for drug use. Coaches and team doctors also may urge athletes to compete despite an injury. Painkillers and other drugs can enable players to participate even when they're hurt. However, this short-term solution can lead to long-term health problems. Despite the risks, athletes often are willing to risk their physical well-being in order to remain competitive.

The Trickle-Down Effect

Just as professional athletes feel ever-increasing pressure to perform, young people participating in sports are continually facing greater expectations. Even elementary school children are pushed by their parents and coaches to excel and win, rather than concentrating on fun and the value of teamwork and sportsmanship. There have been cases where parents of young athletes have assaulted other parents or attempted to sabotage their children's competitors.

The stakes are high enough in high school sports that some student athletes turn to supplements, steroids, and other performance-enhancing drugs. Parents and coaches expect athletes to put in long hours training while balancing schoolwork and other activities. Gifted athletes compete for prestigious sports scholarships. Pressure to fit in is also a factor—the number of teens who take performance-enhancing drugs in order to look better has been increasing.

The University of Michigan administers the Monitoring the Future survey. In 2005, this study on teen behavior and attitudes concerning drugs indicated that 1.8 percent of all U.S. high school seniors had taken steroids within the past twelve months. More than 40 percent of these students reported that they could easily obtain steroids. Many coaches, teachers, and parents acknowledged concern about athletes using supplements and performance-enhancing drugs, but they admitted it was difficult to combat. One reason for this is that a drug test for steroids generally costs more than $100. The high costs mean that most schools cannot afford the widespread testing that would be needed for testing to become a deterrent.

Drugs Used in Sports

Some sports organizations have more extensive lists of banned substances than others. A drug is likely to be prohibited if it poses a health risk to an athlete and gives him or her an unfair advantage over competitors. Deciding to ban a substance is not always a straightforward matter. What about supplements and herbal remedies, for example? And caffeine? Should the favorite stimulant of many Americans be banned?

A booming business exists for illegal steroids and other performance-enhancing drugs. Athletes can often buy these drugs at their gyms, through the Internet, or from unethical doctors, coaches, or teammates. Some black-market drugs are stolen from pharmacies or veterinary supplies. In other cases, drugs are produced by illicit laboratories or smuggled into the United States from other countries. Such illegally obtained chemicals may be counterfeit, or they may be contaminated with other substances. Even when the drugs are the real thing, athletes often take huge doses, which increase health risks.

Anabolic Steroids

Many people, when they think of performance-enhancing drugs, immediately think of steroids, the most notorious doping agent. "Steroids" is a somewhat vague description, however, since steroids are actually a broad class of hormones naturally produced by the body. The specific agents used by athletes are synthetic forms of anabolic-androgenic steroids (AAS), often called just anabolic steroids. More than 100 different anabolic steroids have been developed. (The steroids used to control a patient's inflammation and swelling are another type of steroids called corticosteroids. Their effects are completely different from those of anabolic steroids.)

Anabolic steroids have both anabolic and androgenic effects. Athletes use these steroids for the anabolic effects of growing and building up muscle mass. The anabolic effects cannot be completely separated from the androgenic, or masculinizing, effects such as a deeper voice and increased growth of body hair. Testosterone, the male sex hormone, is an anabolic steroid. Males naturally produce seven times as much testosterone as females.

Although anabolic steroids are best known for their use in boosting physical performance, they also have some medical uses. For example, doctors prescribe anabolic steroids in hormone replacement therapy, for wasting diseases such as AIDS (acquired immunodefi-

Uwe Schmidt, a police director in Berlin, Germany, holds packages of anabolic steroids that were confiscated in a major 2006 raid. The drugs were smuggled into Germany from Thailand, Poland, and Russia.

ciency syndrome) and some forms of cancer, and to induce puberty in boys who are slow to develop. A variety of anabolic steroids are manufactured for veterinary use and are prescribed to help dogs, cats, and horses increase their appetite and gain weight after lengthy illnesses. Some dopers find that these drugs are easier to obtain than steroids manufactured for human consumption.

Steroids can be taken orally in the form of a pill or injected into a muscle. Users often combine different steroids in order to maximize the effect or avoid detection.

They carefully space dosages in regimens lasting from about a month to three months. Typical doses are huge, much larger than those used for medical purposes.

Although steroids bulk up muscle mass, they do not increase strength. In order to benefit from the increased muscle, steroid users must continue or increase their resistance training. Athletes using steroids are able to undertake more rigorous workouts without the toll on muscles that would occur without steroid use.

The Health Risks of Steroids

Since athletes often lie about their steroid use, it is difficult for researchers to gauge the full extent of side effects—both long-term and short-term—from repeated steroid users. It is known, however, that the drugs have a number of dangerous side effects, some of which can cause permanent damage or even be fatal. Even young, otherwise healthy athletes are at risk. Many users injure tendons and ligaments that are connected to muscles. Steroids can affect blood cholesterol levels and trigger cardiovascular diseases such as heart attack, stroke, and an enlarged heart. Steroids also can damage the liver, which processes drugs once they enter the body. Users may develop liver conditions such as jaundice, hepatitis, or cirrhosis. The kidneys, prostate, and reproductive system also may suffer adverse effects.

In addition, steroid use changes the body's hormone balance, causing a variety of side effects. Women may experience changes such as increased growth of body hair, male pattern baldness, and a deeper voice. These symptoms are sometimes irreversible. Men, on the other hand, may experience shrinkage of the testicles and may develop enlarged breasts, a result of some testosterone being converted into the female sex hormone estradiol. Adolescents using steroids risk stunting their height, since high levels of testosterone can fool the body into triggering a premature end to bone growth.

The psychological side effects of steroid use can be significant. The most controversial aspect is the heightened aggression, known as 'roid rage, that may occur. Although studies have not been able to show a direct link between testosterone and violent outbursts, it is believed that steroid use is linked with an increased risk of severe mood swings, manic behavior, and depression. Some researchers also believe that steroids are psychologically addictive.

Other Doping Substances

Athletes may combine steroids with other drugs in order to further boost the effects, mask detection, or minimize side effects. Depending on an athlete's sport, a variety of other drugs can be taken to enhance performance in specific ways.

Human Growth Hormone

Human growth hormone (HGH), naturally produced by the pituitary gland, stimulates growth during childhood and adolescence. Synthetic HGH was developed to treat patients with conditions such as hormone deficiency. Athletes take HGH or related compounds to promote muscle development and cartilage growth. Adverse side effects include abnormal growth of bones in the face and enlargement of the liver and some other organs. Use of HGH to enhance performance is a fairly new phenomenon, so little is known about long-term effects. Since HGH is produced naturally in the body, it is very hard to detect through drug tests.

Erythropoietin

Like HGH, erythropoietin (EPO) is a naturally occurring hormone. The kidneys produce EPO in response to low levels of oxygen in blood circulation. EPO then triggers the production of red blood cells, which raises the overall oxygen-carrying capacity of the blood. In the 1980s, a synthetic form of EPO was developed to treat anemia, and athletes soon started using it as a performance-enhancing drug. For endurance athletes such as runners, cyclists, and cross-country skiers, increased red blood cell levels translate to greater respiratory capacity of the muscles. One grave danger of EPO is that it thickens the blood, causing the heart to work harder. A number of high-profile cyclists have died of heart failure attributed to EPO use, including Belgian amateur cyclist Johan Sermon and 1998 Tour de France winner Marco Pantani.

Blood Doping

The illicit practice of raising an athlete's levels of red blood cells before competition is called blood doping; therefore, EPO is a blood-doping agent. An athlete can achieve the same effects through blood transfusions. Months before a competition, blood is removed from the athlete's body. The red blood cells are separated out and frozen. The body replenishes the blood that was removed. Then, just before the event, the additional red blood cells are transferred directly into the athlete's bloodstream, significantly raising his or her red-blood-cell level.

Stimulants

Stimulants work by exciting the central nervous system, thereby activating the body's "fight-or-flight" response. Heart rate and blood pressure increase, and the eyes' pupils become dilated (enlarged). The user feels strong, alert, and full of energy. Athletes take stimulants for their exhilarating effects and to combat the fatigue often

Scientist Stephen Kauffman works in a California lab that provides testing for the National Center for Drug Free Sport. In this photo, he examines a digital image of an EPO test, looking for patterns that would indicate banned red-blood-cell boosters.

resulting from grueling schedules. Amphetamine is one of the most popular stimulants among athletes, along with cocaine, methamphetamine, and ephedrine. Stimulants can have a range of serious side effects, including addiction and overtaxation of the cardiovascular system.

Diuretics

Diuretics are drugs that cause users to lose "water weight" from their bodies by increasing urine production. Athletes trying to reach a minimum weight—such as wrestlers or jockeys—may use diuretics immediately before a competition. The effect of diuretics is temporary, so the fluid balance in the body is quickly restored. Some diuretics may lower blood pressure, but not to a dangerous extent. Athletes taking other doping agents may use diuretics before taking a drug test, hoping to avoid detection by diluting and increasing urine output.

Beta Blockers

Beta blockers are drugs that block some effects of the body's fight-or-flight response. They can reduce the pounding heart rate and trembling hands often caused by nerves before a competition. For this reason, athletes who require coordination and steady hands, like archers or marksmen, sometimes use them. Bowlers, golfers, divers, billiards players, and even musicians and actors have been known to turn to beta blockers to improve performance.

Supplements

Sports and dietary supplements are a huge class of products with varying degrees of risk and effectiveness. Some supplements offer claims of bigger muscles, faster weight loss, greater energy, and improved endurance. Nutritional supplements in the form of powders and drinks provide additional protein and amino acids. Drinks and pills containing caffeine are marketed to boost energy. A host of different herbs, vitamins, and minerals are marketed to improve performance and appearance in various ways.

Although there's a booming market for supplements, not all of them are safe. Since the products' manufacturers, not government agencies, are largely responsible for guaranteeing these substances' safety, any athlete should carefully evaluate his or her needs and do some background research. Critics claim that the lax regulation allows the sale of some dangerous products, as well as ineffective products that are merely a waste of money.

One of the highest-profile examples is the supplement androstenedione. Although the drug's actual effectiveness has not been proven, sales of "andro" soared in 1998 after it became known that hitter Mark McGwire used the supplement during his record-breaking season. Andro is a prohormone, a precursor to a hormone— about 5 percent is converted into testosterone in the body. In 2004, the Food and Drug Administration (FDA) banned its sale.

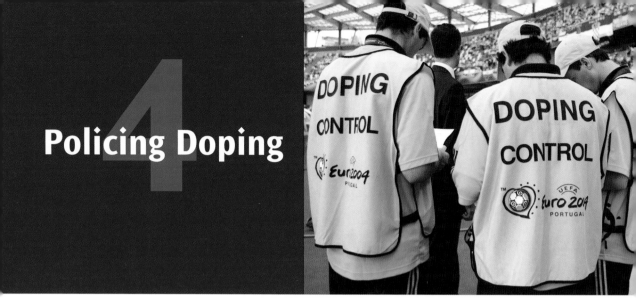

Policing Doping

Nearly every major sport has been plagued by athletes' use of banned substances. Furthermore, it is likely that there will always be athletes willing to go outside the rules and even the law in order to become or stay competitive. Athletes who use performance-enhancing drugs may start for any number of reasons, from a desire to increase their performance quickly to a belief that steroids and other drugs will speed their recovery from injuries. By attempting to give themselves an edge through the use of drugs, dopers bypass the hard work and practice required to stay competitive through their natural abilities. This is why to most other athletes and to many fans, doping is considered cheating. Athletes who use performance-enhancing drugs to advance their careers essentially render meaningless the efforts of honest athletes. The health risks and side effects of doping provide further reasons for banning performance-enhancing drugs and testing athletes to prevent their use.

When an athlete is suspected of doping, the only way to prove or disprove the charge is through testing. Testing, particularly random testing, should be enough of a deterrent to keep athletes clean and honest. Theoretically, the threat of testing positive, then being publicly exposed as a cheater and punished, should outweigh any advantages that a player may gain through doping.

The Integrity of Competition

Cheating has long been an aspect of competitive sports. In baseball, for example, this happens whenever a hitter uses a corked bat or a pitcher doctors a baseball by marring its surface. In track and field, it may happen if a runner elbows other competitors. Whatever the sport, there's often some way to either gain an advantage or hinder an opponent by going outside the rules. Sometimes the player or competitor is caught and disciplined, sometimes not.

Still, teams and competitors can be trained to watch out for cheating. There's often physical evidence on the field or it's captured on video. With performance-enhancing drugs, however, there's often only the suspicion that an athlete is doping. A runner may suddenly and inexplicably become faster than ever before, or a baseball player who hasn't hit many home runs may start crushing the ball.

Of course, honest athletes have outstanding performances in which they set records or surpass their previous statistics. Because of doping, those remarkable performances by honest athletes also may become suspect. In this way, athletes who use performance-enhancing drugs inadvertently deny honest athletes the chance to bask in their accomplishments.

Athletes who use performance-enhancing drugs severely damage the reputation of their respective sports in the eyes of fans. A favorite athlete's positive drug test can be a tremendous blow to anyone who had admired him or her. When Baltimore Orioles outfielder Rafael Palmeiro briefly returned to baseball after his 2005 suspension for a positive steroids test, the booing from the stands was so loud that the formerly beloved player had to wear earplugs. Whether they like it or not, athletes are role models to millions of people, many of them children and teenagers. Unfortunately, a desire to be like a particular athlete may lead to a young person's use of steroids.

Doping and the Law

The international community has attempted to regulate steroids for almost as long as they have existed. The Council of Europe—an organization of twenty-one

Western European nations—banned doping in 1960. The International Olympic Committee (IOC) started testing athletes in 1968, and full-scale testing of all Olympic competitors began in 1972. The IOC officially banned competitors from using anabolic steroids in 1975. Since then, the list of banned substances has expanded to include more than forty different drugs and drug classifications.

In 1957, in an effort to reduce steroid use, the American Medical Association (AMA) established a group now called the Committee on the Medical Aspects of Sports. Apart from the Olympics and other international competitions, however, the United States didn't move to criminalize doping until the 1980s. Scandals such as the Pittsburgh cocaine trials of 1985 and college football star Brian Bosworth's 1986 suspension for steroid use finally prodded the government to address a growing problem.

In 1988, the U.S. House of Representatives made it a federal crime to manufacture, sell, or use anabolic steroids for non-medical use. The Anabolic Steroid Control Act of 1990 went even further, setting steep fines for the sale or possession of anabolic steroids. At the time, the law categorized twenty-seven steroids as Schedule III controlled substances, the same classification as drugs such as cocaine and heroin. The Anabolic Steroid Control Act of 2004 updated this law. In addition, many states have enacted their own laws regulating steroids.

BALCO founder Victor Conte with a photograph of Barry Bonds. Bonds, who allegedly used drugs from the company, wears a hat with the letters "ZMA," a BALCO drug.

BALCO and the Effectiveness of Anti-Doping Laws

The federal investigation that began with the 2003 BALCO raid continues to raise questions about the effectiveness of U.S. anti-doping laws. The BALCO case involved prominent athletes in many sports, particularly baseball, football, and track and field. During his grand jury testimony, BALCO client Jason Giambi allegedly stated that he hadn't worried about testing because he only used steroids during baseball's off-season. The fallout from the BALCO scandal may result in criminal perjury charges for Barry Bonds if it is found that he lied under oath when he denied knowingly taking steroids.

Others involved in BALCO have already served time in jail, including trainer Greg Anderson and BALCO owner Victor Conte. Both pleaded guilty to charges of steroid distribution and money laundering. Each served four months in prison. Since completing his sentence, Anderson has returned to prison twice on charges of contempt for refusing to testify against Barry Bonds. Mark Fainaru-Wada and Lance Williams, the two *San Francisco Chronicle* reporters who broke the BALCO story, have been jailed for refusing to name the source that leaked Barry Bonds's grand jury testimony. They were released after the source revealed himself.

Anti-Doping Policies in U.S. Professional Sports

The criteria established by the IOC are widely considered the gold standard in anti-doping policy. In the United States, however, anti-doping policies vary from sport to sport. USA Track and Field, for example, the governing body that oversees all of the country's track and field competitions, follows the same standards as the IOC. Athletes are tested after each race. A positive test is followed by a second test. If the second test is also positive, the athlete can be subjected to a two-year ban from the sport. If an athlete is caught a second time, the ban becomes a lifetime ban. Despite the harsh penalties, athletes such as Justin Gatlin and Tim Montgomery were not deterred from using steroids.

Baseball's anti-doping policy has become tougher than what it was, but its policy is far less severe than that of other sports. Players caught for a first offense are suspended for fifty games. They are suspended for 100 games if they're caught again, and banned for life if they test positive a third time. The policy calls for players to submit to testing throughout the season (players are tested during their spring training physicals, and there is random testing throughout the season and off-season). Though steroids and other illegal drugs are on the list of banned substances, loopholes mean that players may use undetectable drugs like HGH and insulin.

The National Football League (NFL) has tested players for steroids since 1987, making its doping policy the oldest in U.S. professional sports. For a first-time offense, the NFL suspends players for four games. Suspensions increase to a full year for a second positive test. In a league that plays only sixteen games a year, a four-game suspension can be significant, and a suspension of a year or more could permanently damage a player's career. In addition, under guidelines adopted on January 24, 2007, players will be tested more frequently and will face harsher financial penalties. Still, the NFL policy is criticized by some as being lenient, since it doesn't call for a player to be permanently banned after multiple positive tests.

In the National Basketball Association (NBA), the first positive test for steroids leads to a ten-game suspension. The penalty is increased to twenty-five games for the second positive test, and a full season for a third. A fourth positive test results in dismissal from the league.

The LPGA will start testing its athletes for performance-enhancing drugs in 2008. In golf and other sports that require steady hands, these drugs include beta blockers and others that calm nerves.

Some professional golfers will soon be subjected to drug testing to prevent doping. The Ladies Professional Golfing Association (LPGA) has announced that mandatory testing for its athletes will begin in 2008.

U.S. College and High School Anti-Doping Policies

In college sports, the National Collegiate Athletic Association (NCAA) manages drug testing. All college sports' participants are subject to testing. If an athlete tests positive for performance-enhancing drugs, he or she is suspended from all team activities for a full year. Many schools also have their own penalties for the use of performance-enhancing drugs. Some, like the University of North Carolina, have a zero-tolerance policy. The first time an athlete tests positive for steroids, he or she is banned from all of the school's athletic programs.

In 2006, after a New Jersey health department study showed that high schoolers' steroid use had increased from 3 percent in 1995 to 5 percent in 2001, the state became the first in the country to announce that it would begin testing high school athletes for steroids. Other U.S. states, including Maryland, Florida, California, and Texas, have moved to adopt programs designed to address steroid use, though many struggle with the idea of making testing mandatory. (Civil liberty advocates, in particular, argue that mandatory testing of high school athletes would be an invasion of their privacy.) A state law proposed in Texas would call for random testing of all of the state's high school athletes. If approved, it would be the largest high school testing program in the nation. Even without state laws specifically addressing steroids in schools, steroid users could face serious consequences by violating federal laws, as well as their school district's anti-drug policy.

The Future of Doping

S ince the 1950s, when steroids were first produced in a laboratory, researchers have manufactured dozens of variations of the drugs. For the athletes willing to risk their health and careers, steroid manufacturers are constantly working to find new ways to beat drug tests. Doping critics warn that steroid researchers may soon develop new batches of undetectable drugs, voiding many recent anti-doping policies and further damaging the public image of athletes.

Keeping Up with the Cheaters

In 2003, the U.S. Anti-Doping Agency became aware of a new "designer" steroid called tetrahydrogestrinone, or THG. This drug, a modified version of a common black-market steroid, was developed specifically to cheat drug tests. Scientists quickly devised a test for the substance, and a number of prominent athletes reportedly tested positive for use of the drug. THG was added to a number of banned drug lists.

The discovery of THG highlights the difficulty of policing performance-enhancing drugs in an age where medical and scientific knowledge is constantly evolving. Anti-doping organizations must constantly be on the alert for other designer steroids and new drugs developed to boost performance and avoid detection.

New medical breakthroughs could also bring about a next generation of doping agents. Gene therapy, for example, which involves the modification of a patient's DNA, may someday provide cures for genetic diseases. Progress made in genetic research has caused some people to speculate about "gene doping" becoming a possibility in the future. Hypothetically, an athlete could have a gene inserted or replaced that would boost physical performance. Stem cell research, which has the potential to advance cures for a variety of medical conditions, could be abused by providing ways of enhancing an athlete's natural abilities. Since illicit means of performance enhancement cannot be regulated for safety, it is likely that such new developments would be even more dangerous than doping substances used today.

As diligently as sports organizations may work to eliminate doping, the dopers are often at least one step ahead of the regulators. In the BALCO case, the laboratory had been selling steroids to athletes for years. Federal investigators didn't raid the company until they had been tipped off to the nature of its business by track and field coach Trevor Graham, who coached Marion Jones and has been linked to several doping scandals. When investigators searched BALCO owner Victor Conte's house, they discovered a list of clients and dosage plans for each one. Conte, in turn, accused Graham of distributing an oral testosterone to his athletes that was undetectable within a week of discontinuing use. Such drugs, if in existence, likely would be very tricky to detect. Regulators worry that other undetectable drug compounds may be around the corner.

Sportsmanship in the Twenty-First Century

The use of performance-enhancing drugs in sports is one issue in a society that is fixated on physical perfection. Actors and entertainers set an unrealistic ideal body image that leads to many people's dissatisfaction with their own perceived imperfections. Americans are increasingly turning to cosmetic surgery and other procedures to extend their youth or "improve" their appearances. Adolescents and even younger children may form a negative self-image and try to change their looks through dieting and other means. One danger of this attitude is the chance that the public will gradually grow more accepting of performance-enhancing drugs,

Despite widespread doping allegations, professional baseball players and other athletes continue to attract young fans who look up to them as role models. "Clean" players set a positive example for fans.

thinking that it isn't much different from already accepted ways of changing physical appearance. On the contrary, it's important that athletes and sports fans take a stand against the use of steroids and other dangerous doping substances.

Athletes as Positive Role Models

Young people look up to athletes as role models. Professional athletes can play an important role in discouraging doping by providing a positive example. Aspiring athletes are more likely to listen to warnings against drug use if their heroes are not involved in doping scandals. Although top athletes may feel incredible pressure to put forth winning performances and break records, they must be persuaded that any possible benefits of performance-enhancing drugs are not worth the risk. Athletes can have impressive careers without resorting to doping. Until this happens, anti-doping policies must continue, and sporting organizations need to be attentive in order to keep up with the dopers.

Doping Is Not the Answer

Parents, coaches, and teachers must actively promote the value of sportsmanship and work to create a positive experience for all young people participating in athletics. Even with youngsters, adults have the tendency to push athletes to perform aggressively and win. It is essential that young athletes are educated about the importance of an overall healthy lifestyle and the dangers of performance-enhancing drugs. They must learn that real athletic success comes from hard work and practice, not from a drug produced in a laboratory.

Glossary

allegation An assertion, especially relating to misconduct or wrongdoing, that is made without proof.

amphetamines A group of drugs that act as a stimulant of the central nervous system.

anabolic Characterized by or promoting constructive metabolism, such as the building up of muscles.

androgenic Possessing or promoting masculine characteristics.

anemia A condition in which there are too few red blood cells, or the red blood cells lack in hemoglobin, an iron-containing protein.

biathlon An athletic competition consisting of cross-country skiing and rifle shooting events.

black market The illicit buying and selling of goods.

Botox Botulinum toxin, a treatment increasingly used in cosmetic procedures to flatten wrinkles.

cardiovascular Relating to or affecting the heart and blood vessels.

cartilage A tough, elastic connective tissue found in the joints and other parts of the body.

cocaine An addictive narcotic drug taken as a stimulant.

Cold War A period of hostility and indirect conflict in the mid-twentieth century between the United States and the Soviet Union.

corticosteroids Steroid hormones produced by the adrenal cortex, or their synthetic equivalents. These are not the same as anabolic-androgenic steroids used to enhance athletic performance.

deterrent Something that discourages action or prevents something from happening.

digitalis A drug, obtained from the plant foxglove, that acts as a cardiac stimulant.

DNA Deoxyribonucleic acid, a type of molecule that encodes genetic information.

endurance Stamina; in athletics, especially the ability to exercise for long periods of time.

erythropoietin (EPO) A hormone that promotes the production of red blood cells.

ethics A set of moral principles.

genetic Involving or relating to genes, the basic units of hereditary characteristics.

hormone A substance produced by the body that regulates functions such as growth and metabolism.

human growth hormone (HGH) The hormone secreted by the pituitary gland that promotes body growth.

illicit Illegal or unauthorized.

implicated Involved in; had close connection to an activity.

indict To formally charge somebody with a crime or wrongdoing.

innocuous Producing no ill effects; harmless.

insulin A naturally occurring hormone secreted from the pancreas that controls the blood glucose level.

lenient Showing tolerance and compassion in dealing with misbehavior or crime.

nitroglycerine A chemical used medically to treat heart conditions.

pentathlete An athlete competing in a pentathlon, five different track and field events.

prohormone An inactive precursor to a hormone.

resistance training A form of exercise intended to strengthen the muscles.

stamina Strength of physical constitution.

steroids (anabolic-androgenic steroids, or AAS) A class of hormones that promote growth, particularly of muscle and bone.

stimulant A substance that produces a temporary increase in the function, activity, or efficiency of an organism.

strychnine A poisonous chemical that acts as a stimulant of the central nervous system.

subpoena A written legal order summoning a witness or requiring evidence to be submitted to court.

synthetic Produced artificially by humans.

tendon A cord of tough, inelastic tissue that connects muscle and bone.

testosterone The male sex hormone.

For More Information

International Olympic Committee
Château de Vidy
1007 Lausanne
Switzerland
Web site: http://www.olympic.org

National Center for Drug Free Sport, Inc.
2537 Madison Avenue
Kansas City, MO 64108
(816) 474-8655
Web site: http://www.drugfreesport.com

National Strength and Conditioning Association (NSCA)
1885 Bob Johnson Drive
Colorado Springs, CO 80906
(800) 815-6826 or (719) 632-6722
Web site: http://www.nsca.com

SAMHSA's National Clearinghouse for Alcohol and
    Drug Information
P.O. Box 2345
Rockville, MD 20847-2345
(800) 729-6686
Web site: http://ncadi.samhsa.gov

United States Anti-Doping Agency (USADA)
1330 Quail Lake Loop, Suite 260
Colorado Springs, CO 80906-4651
(866) 601-2632 or (719) 785-2000
Web site: http://www.usantidoping.org

World Anti-Doping Agency (WADA)
Stock Exchange Tower
800 Place Victoria, Suite 1700
P.O. Box 120
Montreal, QC H4Z 1B7
Canada
(514) 904-9232
Web site: http://www.wada-ama.org

Web Sites

Due to the changing nature of Internet links, Rosen
Publishing has developed an online list of Web sites
related to the subject of this book. This site is updated
regularly. Please use this link to access the list:

http://www.rosenlinks.com/itn/daad

For Further Reading

Bahrke, Michael S., and Charles E. Yesalis, eds. *Performance-Enhancing Substances in Sport and Exercise.* Champaign, IL: Human Kinetics, 2002.

Beamish, Rob, and Ian Ritchie. *Fastest, Highest, Strongest: A Critique of High-Performance Sport.* New York, NY: Routledge, 2006.

Connolly, Sean. *Steroids* (Just the Facts). Chicago, IL: Heinemann Library, 2001.

Egendorf, Laura K. *Performance-Enhancing Drugs.* San Diego, CA: Referencepoint Press, 2007.

Fitzhugh, Karla. *Steroids* (What's the Deal?). Chicago, IL: Heinemann Library, 2006.

Gifford, Clive. *Drugs and Sports* (Face the Facts). Chicago, IL: Raintree, 2003.

Lazell, Marguerite. *Tour de France: The Illustrated History.* Buffalo, NY: Firefly Books, 2003.

Bibliography

Associated Press. "Texas Bill Would Create Largest Steroid Testing Program." Espn.com. March 3, 2007. Retrieved March 28, 2007 (http://sports.espn.go.com/sports/highschool/news/story?id=2791228).

Bryant, Howard. *Juicing the Game*. New York, NY: Viking, 2005.

Carroll, Will. *The Juice: The Real Story of Baseball's Drug Problems*. Chicago, IL: Ivan R. Dee, 2005.

Fainaru-Wada, Mark, and Lance Williams. *Game of Shadows: Barry Bonds, BALCO, and the Steroids Scandal That Rocked Professional Sports*. New York, NY: Gotham Books, 2006.

Dudley, William, ed. *Drugs and Sports* (At Issue). San Diego, CA; Greenhaven Press, 2000.

Egendorf, Laura K., ed. *Steroids.* Detroit, MI: Greenhaven Press, 2006.

Hoberman, John. *Testosterone Dreams: Rejuvenation, Aphrodisia, Doping*. Berkeley, CA: University of California Press, 2005.

Kuhn, Cynthia, Ph.D., Scott Swartzwelder, Ph.D., and Wilkie Wilson, Ph.D. *Pumped: Straight Facts for Athletes About Drugs, Supplements, and Training*. New York, NY: W. W. Norton & Company, Inc., 2000.

Major League Baseball Player's Association. "MLBPA, MLB Announce New Drug Agreement." November 15, 2005. Retrieved April 10, 2007 (http://mlbplayers.mlb.com/pa/releases/releases.jsp?content=111505).

McCloskey, John, and Julian Bailes, M.D. *When Winning Costs Too Much: Steroids, Supplements, and Scandal in Today's Sports*. New York, NY: Taylor Trade Publishing, 2005.

Monroe, Judy. *Steroids, Sports, and Body Image: The Risks of Performance-Enhancing Drugs* (Issues in Focus). Berkeley Heights, NJ: Enslow Publishers, Inc., 2004.

Reiss, Mike. "NFL Strengthens Drug Policy." *Boston Globe*. January 25, 2007. Retrieved April 10, 2007 (http://www.boston.com/sports/articles/2007/01/25/nfl_strengthens_drug_policy/).

Index

About the Author

Jason Porterfield has written more than twenty books for Rosen Publishing. Several of his previous books have focused on topics related to sports, including *Baseball: Rules, Tips, Strategy, and Safety* and *Kurt Busch: NASCAR Driver*. He graduated from Oberlin College in 2001 with majors in English, history, and religion. He currently lives in Chicago.

Photo Credits

Cover (top left) © Mark Wilson/Getty Images; cover (top right) © Fayez Nureldine/AFP/Getty Images; cover (bottom) © Andy Lyons/Getty Images; p. 4 © Justin Sullivan/Getty Images; p. 7 © Elsa/Getty Images; p. 10 © Gerald Herbert-Pool/Getty Images; p. 14 © Keystone/Getty Images; pp. 15, 20, 27, 28, 37, 44 © AP Image; p. 18 © Romeo Gacad/AFP/Getty Images; p. 22 © Topham/The Image Works; p. 24 © Allsport UK/Allsport/Getty Images; pp. 30, 32 © Sean Gallup/Getty Images; p. 40 © Andreas Rentz/ Bongarts/Getty Images; p. 47 © Robert Laberge/Getty Images; p. 49 © Ian Waldie/Getty Images; p. 52 © Doug Pensinger/Getty Images.

Designer: Tom Forget; **Photo Researcher:** Amy Feinberg